Work and Love

*Ugliest typography
of the year*

*Chatty form ~ casual, prosaic.
Mundane in content,
quotidian anecdotes of
MY (emphasis on speaking self)
life.*

Books by Stephen Dunn

WORK AND LOVE

poems by

Stephen Dunn

Carnegie-Mellon University Press
Pittsburgh 1981
Feffer and Simons, Inc., London

ACKNOWLEDGMENTS

Some of these poems have appeared in:

The American Scholar, Antaeus: "In The San Bernardinos,"
Brahma, The Chowder Review, Crazy Horse, The Georgia Review:
"Because We Are Not Taken Seriously," "Coming On," "The Universe
Is Too Big To Love," The Hiram Poetry Review, The Iowa Review,
The Massachusetts Review: "My Brother's Work," reprinted by
permission; ©1980 The Massachessets Review, Inc., The Missouri
Review, New England Review, New Jersey Poetry Journal,
New Letters, The New Yorker: "That Saturday Without a Car"
reprinted by permission; ©1980 The New Yorker Magazine, Inc.,
Northwest Review, The Ohio Review: "A Worker's Creed,"
"Watching The News," "With No Experience In Such Matters,"
"Having Lost All Capacity," "The Rain Falling Now," Pequod,
Poetry: "Welcome," "Work," "The Photograph In The Hallway,"
"At The Film Society" (originally titled "Movie Night"), "Fairy Tales,"
"Workers," "Elementary Poem," Poetry Northwest, Prairie Schooner:
"Solitude" (originally titled "The House of Solitude"), ©1978
University of Nebraska Press, Quarterly West, raccoon, Vegetable
Box, and Water Table.

My thanks to Yaddo for its support.

And for grants from the New Jersey State Council on the Arts and
Stockton State College.

The publication of this book is supported by grants from the
National Endowment for the Arts in Washington, D.C., a Federal
agency, and from the Pennsylvania Council on the Arts.

CONTENTS

III

For Joe Rubenstein

For one human being to love another: that is perhaps the most difficult of our tasks, the ultimate, the last test and proof, the work for which all other work is but preparation.

—Rilke

I am labor, I am a disposition to live.

—David Ignatow

I

FIVE PRELUDES:

Violence

1. Watching The News

"She would have been a good woman
if there had been somebody there
to shoot her every minute of her life."
—From Flannery O'Connor's
"A Good Man Is Hard To Find"

Weeping can be dull, but the weeper
doesn't care about what's interesting.
She just turns every room
into a blue room, helplessly.
We must not watch her
though the pornographer in us
edges closer, turns up the sound.
Her children dead, her husband maimed,
the newsman thinks it's journalism
to ask how she feels.
Oh newsman, all this violence and still
I'd like to shoot you now, maybe
just in the hand or leg
so I could shoot you again tomorrow.
Let there be amendments against
such free speech. And when
the Nazis want to march again
let us be clear and negative
—and for liberalism, a whiff of gas.
For us, a turning away now;
a need for some grace
for what is graceless in us,
some help for our inexact hearts
cocked and about to go off
every minute of our lives.

2. The Trial

I scatter stones and twigs
until there's a surface
I can live on. The pegs go in
easily, by nightfall I've forgotten
the marketplace and it has
forgotten me. The Coleman is lit,
the mixed aroma, yes,
of woods and night and cold.
Here now is a place
for some final displacement—
where I might go
if and when the small things
which are my life reveal themselves
to be simply what they are.
This is just a trial, a see-if-I-can,
I'll try it for two days,
two nights . . .
I imagine the special loneliness
of being searched for
when I know where I am.
I imagine causing grief
and taking grief's measurements,
learning all the hidden costs.
And when I come back
like some hello that insinuates
it wants to stay the night,
she will have discovered
she can live without me
and her love will become strangely generous,
free, unobliged.
            That's how I see it, here
with the tent flaps open, the eyes
of animals all around.
Somewhere an owl who-ing into the dark.
And closer than ever, like deception,
the ancient promises of the stars.

3. Dream Story

I'm the fourth in a line of four men.
We're waiting for things
to open up. I was originally fifth

but the fourth man died
when Jean Luc Godard stabbed him
for political reasons. I moved up.

The man behind the window is a reflection
of how things are. He's taking his time,
cleaning his fingernails with a fingernail

on his other hand. One nail therefore
is always dirty, the problem eternal.
The third man has a secret tucked under

his arm. He's so thin I can almost see it
protruding from the spot where the bicep
lies flat against the bone. And if I could

see it, I might know why I'm standing here
amid such solemnity, no one
to turn to. I start to sing jambalaya

and a crawfish pie and a fillet gumbo.
I wrinkle cellophane
to test the patience of the third man

whose secret begins to slip, obscenely,
into sunlight. The second man
seems to have disappeared

because the *auteur* wanted him to.
I'm third now.
Each of us seems to know

that anything can happen, that his position
earned by simple industry
is subject to the whims of injustice.

4. Having Lost All Capacity

Violence

Taxi Driver

"I am a man and count
nothing human alien to me."
—Terence

Today I read how Japanese fishermen
lured thousands of dolphins ashore,
slaughtering them because they eat fish
the fishermen want to catch and sell,
and tomorrow it'll be people once again
mutilating other people, and there'll come a time
when I'll just sit there turning the pages
having lost all capacity for horror
and so much that is human
will be alien to me I'll want to kill
all the killers, I'll walk past my wife
with a kitchen knife and out the door
into streets where others like me
will be slashing at wind and shadows . . .
until the first ripped neck.

I hear everything gets calmer then.
After the first time with a girl I remember
smelling my fingers and then tasting them,
and that's what I hear the first righteous
murder smells and tastes like, only better,
and with the headlines from a week of tabloids
in my mouth I'll know what the end
of the world tastes like, *irresistible*,
and that's all I can think about
here in my room, the sons of bitches,
the bastards!

5. Expectations

On any given day
fallen exhaust pipes
like cobras peering up
from the sides of roads,
the scattered rubber of blow-outs,
here and there a crow
on a white dividing line
eating the ripped daylights
of a possum. Country, city,
it doesn't matter,
things shoot out at you
or are about to collapse
the entire time.
Even here, indoors,
no escape from it:
names to erase,
the natural debris of love.
The good in goodbye,
the hell in hello,
on any given day
whole words falling apart, too.

WELCOME

If you believe nothing is always what's left
after a while, as I did,
If you believe you have this collection
of ungiven gifts, as I do (right here
behind the silence and the averted eyes)
If you believe an afternoon can collapse
into strange privacies—
how in your backyard, for example,
the shyness of flowers can be suddenly
overwhelming, and in the distance
the clear goddamn of thunder
personal, like a voice,
If you believe there's no correct response
to death, as I do; that even in grief
(where I've sat making plans)
there are small corners of joy
If your body sometimes is a light switch
in a house of insomniacs
If you can feel yourself straining
to be yourself every waking minute
If, as I am, you are almost smiling . . .

CHECKLIST

The housework, the factory work, the work
that takes from the body
and does not put back.
The white collar work and the dirt
of its profits, the terrible politeness
of the officeworker, the work that robs
the viscera to pay the cool
surfaces of the brain. All the work
that makes love difficult, brings on
sleep, drops the body off
at the liquor cabinet. All the work
that reaches the intestines and sprawls.
And the compulsive work after the work
is done, those unfillable spaces
of the Calvinist, or certain marriage beds.

MY BROTHER'S WORK

My brother who knows
the indignity of work
rides home with the taste of it
turning peptic, that odor
of swallowed pride rising
into his breath, his wife waiting
for the kiss that's so full
of the day she can't bear it.
My brother who hears the shout
of bosses, who is no boss himself,
only shouts at home,
thinks shouting is what permits
the bosses to move
with the easy self-
fulfilled gait of leopards
who've eaten all they've killed.
My brother who will not leave
his job wonders how Gauguin left
the world and found himself
on the other side of it.
"What *balls*," he says; "braver
than a suicide." My brother
who is no less than anyone
circumstance has made
to do its bidding, who wants
to rise one morning against
all odds and slip
into his leopard body,
my brother is
coming home now and his wife
is waiting for the kiss.

LOVE:

Hard work, the experts say.
Needs a man with a mind
for redefinitions, a woman
with prior experience.
Or any combination thereof.

Far away from such pap,
you underline *all that's ripe*
must die soon, and leave the book
open for me to see it.
Now our hands begin to move
to remove what separates us.
We're feeling it, that need
to suck and succumb,
anything else is liquor
diluted, is love spoken about
from an armchair by someone
settled in, and down. Love,
let's remember this moment.
        As I touch you
some magnificent apple grown perfect
beyond endurance is falling.

SOLITUDE

Sometimes it's unbearable—
each of us a star
burning in a different galaxy,
breathing different air,
no nourishment equal to our need

to consume. Tonight, though,
I take the fine solitude you bring
and mix it with my own.
What I give back is garnished
with privacy,

your favorite food,
rich as a truffle
grown underground for years.
To give and receive like this—
each sharing what each

can barely afford—this is
the coming together I love.
I pour the little wine
we've left, and we click
our glasses and nod.

When the unspeakable rises up,
perches on the tip
amidst all that's sayable and good,
we move closer, do something else
with our tongues.

ODYSSEUS AT RUSH HOUR

Now evening with its simple
exclusions puts afternoon
to bed, and driving home
I feel my blood pick up
a little speed as if the bloodstream
were where the wind goes
after it dies.
This is the other world
between the half-life of work
and the half-life of home;
it's why so many men stop at bars,
it's why so many women out shopping
for new lives cancel dinner
and walk off by themselves.
Tonight I want to prolong all arrivals.
I want to be perpetually alive
in the tense air
that surrounded Einstein
moments before $E=MC^2$.
Once, on my girlfriend's birthday,
I tied a ribbon in a bow
around my penis and waited
for her to find it.
I had to stay soft. I had to wait
better than I had ever waited.
Red lights, be my friend.
Traffic, slow down.
When I finally turn the key
in my front door
I want to be bringing home a man
who's been away so long
only love can save him,
good excuses be damned.

HARD WORK

1956

At the Coke plant, toting empties
in large crates to the assembly line,
I envied my friends away at camp,
but the money was good
and hard work, my father said,
was how you became a man.
I saw a man for no special reason
piss into a coke bottle
and put it back onto the line.
After a while I, too, hated
the bottles enough to break some
deliberately, and smile
and share with the other workers
a petty act of free will.
When I came home at night my body
hurt with that righteous hurt
men have brought home for centuries,
the hurt that demands
food and solicitation, that makes men
separate, lost.
I quit before the summer was over,
exercised the prerogatives of my class
by playing ball all August
and spent the money I'd earned
on Barbara Winokur, who was beautiful.
And now I think my job
must be phased out, a machine must
do it, though someone for sure
still does the hard work of boredom
and that person can't escape,
goes there each morning
and comes home each night
and probably has no opportunity
to say who he is
through destruction, some big
mechanical eye watching him
or some time and motion man
or just something hesitant, some father
or husband, in himself.

WORKERS

I've seen bees, in the spell of a queen,
mine the clover all afternoon
and ants, those laborers, hauling crumbs
to their elaborate dwellings
and lazy crows waiting
for something to be hit by a car
so the pickings will be easy.
And knowing they have no choice
but to obey the imperatives
of their natures, I've moved on
without judgment to the flies
born to be pests and the purple martins
that eat them, and I've been amazed
by the intelligence behind such work,
what eats what, and how much,
the incredible death-work that is
the life of the universe.

And I've known the human work
that uplifts and cleanses, glassblowers
as miraculous as seeds
which hold the shape of flowers,
ordinary people who rival the ant,
who call forth in emergencies
the cockroach's genius for survival.
And I've seen the crow-people too,
the sloth-people, the hyenas,
have seen the cruelty of nature
and the cruelty of economics
merge and twist into confusion,
and have marvelled at the skunk
and its gorgeous white stripe
and its stink and have wondered
if the outlaw, in the company of outlaws,
planning his next job,
isn't the happiest man alive.

A WORKER'S CREED

From sunlight, the obvious and the lush.
The pleasures of exposure
and the pleasures of covering up
with a straw, broad-brimmed hat.
But I like cloudy days like this
after days like that.
Days I can gather speed
and open my eyes the whole way.
I like images like occluded front,
the aesthetics of sensing my shadow
lost in its own substance.
And I like the inspiration I get
from a sudden coolness,
days I can imagine Icarus thinking
"not today," then doing
a little more work on his wings.

THE PHOTOGRAPH IN THE HALLWAY

For D., "through with love"

You've seen it perhaps in the wrong setting,
a photograph of lovers in a haze
of abandon, everything in the room
background to their special dance.
Lacking nothing else,
what they seem to need is oxygen
though this is the emergency
all of us try to arrive at,
equally breathless and contorted.

We've named it
"Mutual Generosity," two people
stopped in the equipoise
outside of time.
We're not deceived by such bliss;
the lovers have long ago returned
to the difficulties of loving.
Theirs is a moving picture now
subject to cool, inexorable laws.

But to say so is a pettiness.
Let us celebrate the photograph
as it is, which is as it might be
for you, after some straight line
in your life gives way
and luck is there like a net.
Let us stop and imagine it,
our fingers palpitating
as if their tips were missing—
such homelessness and longing in them,
such a desire to be properly lost.

LEAVES

Our fenced-in yard
prevents the wind taking them
to other people, other streets.
And the law, never sympathetic

to burning of any kind,
says do not burn.
So we alternate digging in,
alternate holding the bag.

This is work nobody loves,
no skill, no difficulty.
Yet when the rhythm's right
and all else is well with us

it's tolerable, almost fun,
like familiar sex.
Sometimes a dead mouse
in among the leaves,

sometimes a frozen dog turd.
These are natural jokes,
to be counted on each year.
It's understood between us

what full means
and less than full.
We're constantly pushing down,
making room.

And when we fasten a bag
and carry it to the others
there's a proper heaviness
and shape to it,

a proper feel.
Oh, if things are wrong between us
we hire kids.
We've learned monotonous

has little to do with same.
Once, when love
was what we gave to others,
we insisted the bag be opened wider,

complained about the cold.
And when that mouse turned up
she left it for me to touch,
I left it for her.

AT THE MONASTERY OF WORK AND LOVE

The door is closed. I am the one
who separated certain air
from certain other air, who wanted it
this way. It was perfect how
the male part and the female part
clicked and caught,
how all the other rooms
which all day try to press into this room
had to settle to be themselves.
I'm not alone. Each person
in this house has a door of his own,
and each person a knock and rhythm
to that knock, a public code.
Today, we are all in our rooms.
We have closed our doors to do
our solitary jobs. I love how the hinges
perform, unsung as knuckles.
I love the forthrightness of the knob
and its nipple, the lock.
The door itself: my eunuch and friend.
And the others, well, we will meet
later on, as we always do, in the open room
where such meetings are allowed.
I'll bring the portrait
called "The Door." They, whatever
their solitude has stirred.

AT THE FILM SOCIETY

On the empty walls some of the others
project 8-millimeter versions of themselves
while in the large room with the screen
Liv Ullman touches Max von Sydow
with a lust so deepened by grief
the rest of us feel our miseries
are amateurish, some of us are even elated
to have Bergman for such a friend;
oh come over for dinner, Ingmar,
and make our loneliness exquisite.

The woman sitting next to me, overweight
and beautiful, has been crying
since I took her hand and whispered "slit
wrists, betrayal, viciousness, anything
that Ullman does makes me happy."
I'm not sure why she's crying, but I know
how intimacy begins and it has,
I know that the best sex rises
like a trapped beast from our vacancies,
those openings we never knew were there
until touched. Ullman now
has offered her face to theologians
as proof there is a soul; von Sydow
is looking off to the side, afraid
to let go some bottom of himself.
Later, the woman and I will talk about this
in bed, with pleasure.

How soon the others will get tired
of themselves is always a question.
Each of us has been one of them,
waited our turn, then waited again
for the praise that didn't come
fast or true enough.
Now the discussion on Bergman begins.
Now we can give ourselves.

THE CLARITIES

The clarities at dusk, the ones
a lover pulling the shade knows

before he turns to face the imprecision
of a human face. The street light

coming on, the revelation of brown
as the color of melancholy, and melancholy

the mood that wants visitors
but will settle for the repetition

of a song. Now he turns
and sees her as she might have been

had she had less of this, a little more
of that, what light there is

is enough for the surgery that takes place
at the end of day, or love.

On the street below, traffic building up.
Somewhere an alibi fusing with a wish.

MEDITATION ON TWO THEMES

1   The setting for joy is rarely
where it occurs. That real place,
that bed or playing field, is where
we're stunned and the body is
all fog and disbelief
and we're making animal sounds
or a new kind of silence.
I remember feeling it
afterwards driving home or
the next day waking with it
like sunlight on my face.
I remember calling it joy
over the phone, collecting it
into a single word.

2   Suffering: we all know stories
worse than our own.
But I knew a good place for it—
in the space between two garages,
hidden by bushes.
I was a child then, and once
I stayed there an entire day and night.
I was in pajamas, weeping.
Before long
I knew how much they'd miss me,
how happy I could make them.

3   Last week the wife of a friend
     threw her baby out the window,
     proving that all settings are wrong
     if we are wrong or lost or crazy.
     For her there is no hiding,
     no place to run to.
     Across the street, the park
     is full of skaters.
     Balloons rise above the trees
     and wind, without rudder,
     is once again king.

4   The sky won't stay still;
     this must account
     for its history of blueness.
     I know,
     I've followed a lone scud
     going nowhere at dusk
     and become that scud.
     I've pursued things
     long after they were over.
     Always I wanted someone
     to stop me.
     Isn't joy a kind of stillness
     at the top of something,
     before the long falling?

WORK:

To find a substitute for prayer.
To discover how to say the words
you truly mean. Words like "Here I am,
I'll try not to betray you.
Forgive me when I do."
To extend the list of words—
catamaran, peacock, miracle—
that you'd want to hear if awakening,
bewildered, in a room
ominously full of flowers.
To find someone you love
to say them, who knows their music,
someone who could intuit
on what sargasso the comatose are feeding,
and the unrisen wishes, the depth charges,
inside you. To find that person
and risk reviving the dead reflex
of reverence. To therefore and thereafter
learn how to live with disappointment.
To find the words for it, and rhythm.
To give succor, and to give solace.

THAT SATURDAY WITHOUT A CAR

Ellen Dunn
(1910-1969)

Five miles to my mother's house,
a distance I'd never run.
"I *think* she's dead"
my brother said, and hung up

as if with death
language should be mercifully approximate,
should keep the fact
that would never be fact

at bay. I understood,
and as I ran wondered what words
I might say, and to whom.
I saw myself opening the door—

my brother, both of us, embarrassed
by the sudden intimacy we'd feel.
We had expected it
but we'd expected it every year

for ten: her heart was the best
and worst of her—every kindness
fought its way through damage,
her breasts disappeared

as if the heart itself, for comfort,
had sucked them in.
And I was running better
than I ever had. How different it was

from driving, the way I'd gone
to other deaths—
my body fighting it all off, my heart,
this adequate heart, getting me there.

II

POEM FOR PEOPLE WHO ARE UNDERSTANDABLY TOO BUSY TO READ POETRY

Relax. This won't last long.
Or if it does, or if the lines
make you sleepy or bored,
give in to sleep, turn on
the T.V., deal the cards.
This poem is built to withstand
such things. Its feelings
cannot be hurt. They exist
somewhere in the poet,
and I am far away.
Pick it up any time. Start it
in the middle if you wish.
It is as approachable as melodrama,
and can offer you violence
if it is violence you like. Look,
there's a man on a sidewalk;
the way his leg is quivering
he'll never be the same again.
This is your poem
and I know you're busy at the office
or the kids are into your last good nerve.
Maybe it's sex you've always wanted.
Well, *they lie together*
like the party's unbuttoned coats,
slumped on the bed

waiting for drunken arms to move them.
I don't think you want me to go on;
everyone has his expectations, but this
is a poem for the entire family.
Right now, Budweiser
is dripping from a waterfall,
deodorants are hissing into armpits
of people you resemble,
and *the two lovers are dressing now,*
saying farewell.
I don't know what music this poem
can come up with, but clearly
it's needed. For it's apparent
they will never see each other again
and we need music for this
because there was never music when he or she
left *you* standing on that corner.
You see, I want this poem to be nicer
than life. I want you to look at it
when anxiety zigzags your stomach
and the last tranquilizer is gone
and you need someone to tell you
I'll be here when you want me
like the sound inside a shell.
The poem is saying that to you now.
But don't give up anything for this poem.
It doesn't expect much. It will never say more
than listening can explain.
Just keep it in your attache case
or in your house. And if you're not asleep

by now, or bored beyond sense,
the poem wants you to laugh. Laugh at
yourself, laugh at this poem, at all poetry.
Come on:

Good. Now here's what poetry can do.
Imagine yourself a caterpillar.
There's an awful shrug and, suddenly,
you're beautiful for as long as you live.

III

SOMETHING

A wish for something moral like a wound
pitying the knife
its inability to be pleased or sad.
Or perhaps an afternoon one day a month
when everyone can say why they're ashamed.
Something to end the talk that passes
for talk. Something the lonesome ear,
the starved eye, can take in
like nourishment from the other world
in which, now and then, we've lived.

WITH NO EXPERIENCE IN
SUCH MATTERS

To hold a damaged sparrow
under water until you feel it die
is to know a small something
about the mind; how, for example,
it blames the cat for the original crime,
how it wants praise for its better side.

And yet it's as human
as pulling the plug on your Dad
whose world has turned
to feces and fog, human as . . .
well, let's admit, it's a mild thing
as human things go.

But I felt the one good wing
flutter in my palm—
the smallest protest, if that's what it was.
I ever felt or heard.
Reminded me how my eyelid has twitched,
the need to account for it.
Hard to believe no one notices.

LETTER ABOUT MYSELF TO YOU

To Joe Gillon, age 35,
four weeks to live

Joe,
the other day I tried to get my class
to believe something Keatsian and beautiful
about death. What scholastic rot,
true on cool days far away
from the latest personal taste of it.
Next time photos of Dachau, a little
real blood between the lines.
I used to believe in words, how they could
come together happily, and change.
Now I just pray they don't distort.
Cancer's my sign. See what I mean?
I just wanted to say *cancer*
the way a boy first says shit
in front of his parents. There, it's out.
Listen, I'm four years older than you
with a tennis date at five.
That's not guilt, it's another broken piece
among the puzzle's broken pieces,
it's the silence that comes back
after "Why?" is shouted in an empty room.
I need to know if love's absurd
to you now. Or meaningful, perhaps,
for the first time? Your wife,
do you want to make love to her,
or to everyone else? Do the ethics
of it matter, now, at all?
I need to know if rage helps,
if it feels good to spit
in an invisible eye? If resignation
is as sweet as sitting back
in a jacuzzi with a telephone
and someone due to call?
Here, two thousand miles away,
I feel a tick in my cells;
you've brought out a selfishness, Joe,
please believe is empathy.

I'm writing this in the afternoon,
that time of day I'm most lost.
A wind is blowing insignificantly.
My cat, Peaches, curls on my lap,
humming like an extra heart.
What good are words?
I'm feeling that impotence which wants
a Lazarus to rise
everytime someone loved is sinking.
Rise. Miracle. Heaven.
There, I've said them, sadly,
to make you laugh.

BECAUSE WE ARE NOT
TAKEN SERIOUSLY

Some night I wish they'd knock
on my door, the government men,
looking for the poem of simple truths
recited and whispered among the people.
And when all I give them is silence
and my children are exiled
to the mountains, my wife forced
to renounce me in public,
I'll be the American poet
whose loneliness, finally, is relevant
whose slightest movement
ripples cross-country.

And when the revolution frees me,
its leaders wanting me to become
"Poet of the Revolution," I'll refuse
and keep a list of their terrible reprisals
and all the dark things I love
which they will abolish.
With the ghost of Mandelstam
on one shoulder, Lorca on the other,
I'll write the next poem, the one
that will ask only to be believed
once it's in the air, singing.

INSTRUCTIONS FOR
THE NEXT CENTURY

Instead of spouse say sailing ship,
   instead of dancing say
     ancient ruins.

When you want love
   don't say sailing ship, say
     seven-or-eleven.

When you want music say sacrifice,
   for if you dance
     to that music someone will say

secret police which means
   secret police and you'll be caught
     with all the wrong words.

Say cellar door
   when they take you in. Say it
     until it means something else.

Say whipped cream when you mean
   emptiness, say blue lagoon
     when you mean nightmare.

If all day you've planned to escape
   try to be silent. The most silent
     words are ocean floor.

Say ocean floor, blue lagoon, whipped
   cream over and over;
     you will not escape

but other prisoners might hear you
   and call it sacrifice, which will be
     music to the few who remember.

These are your friends. Say seven-or-eleven
   to them. Hold them in your arms
     and call it ancient ruins.

SELF-PORTRAIT

The reflection of my face
in a cracked plate, a confirmation
of some scar I never earned,
pleases me. The black shirt I wear
as a charm against the world
pleases me too; my head rising
out of it like a moon.
Once I was inseparable
from those faces one finds
on posters selling milk,
pleasing all the people
who never pleased me,
but I am pleased now
when owners of gift shops
follow me down their aisles,
when customs agents
stick their fingers up my ass
hunting for stolen jewels,
pleased to have the face
that here and there
disturbs, the hint of a mask
slightly ripped, beneath it a stone
that would be happy to bleed
in the right hands.

THE UNIVERSE IS TOO BIG TO LOVE

Some nights it's better not to look up there.
    The stars appear broken from certain angles,
        certain imperatives of seeing.

Moods! Moods can alter mathematics.
    If only I believed I were unimportant,
        a speck, as a mystic does,

this heaviness in my chest
    wouldn't matter. I could make friends
        with a pebble.

But I'm both a speck *and* important.
    I'm the right size for love.
        Still, there's no reason

for you, out there turning these pages,
    to care about me.
        When a night falls apart

it reveals more night
    and this is true perhaps
        for only one person at a time.

Soon it will be your turn
    and I will be home reading a book,
        perfectly calm.

AFTER LOSSES

For J.P.

Around the time the livingroom
became unbearable to look at
I took in two cats, a grey and a grey.
It was after the dog died and
the house was getting smaller.
It was after I rowed the small boat
into the seascape on the wall;
after I invented the small boat.
The cats ended all of that, for a while.
I was happy to watch them,
their speed and lassitude,
how when they were asleep
I could touch them awake.

But I began to hear the ho-hum
in each purr. I was witness
to the energy that misplaces itself
until it's gone. Mine, not theirs.
My dream: lying back
with a superficial wound, every hour
a nurse's breast glancing my arm.
Such a nice passivity that finally isn't
a life. Circles everywhere
looked like zeroes to me.

I write this for you
who are surrounded by it now, the stasis
that won't end, these afternoons when
there's nothing to say
and you say it
in order to survive.
I want to tell you it ends,
it just goes away.
I remember a twitch in a vein—
as if something lost were tapping on a wall—
no, it wasn't that mystical.
I remember something like joy
coming with a fat pillow of its own . . .
no, it ends,
it just goes away.

TEMPORARILY

The good, true enough stories
about the gods were gone forever—
the universe now was blue and invisible
and at night the stars
little more than a habit.
So when I woke and dressed

and walked out into the morning
I pretended the street rose up
to meet me. I met the facades,
the familiar hazards, eye-level.
Someone slim in knee boots
reminded me of the sexual collision

which for a moment or two
changes the world.
But a sign on a gas pump
cut to the heart:
"Temporarily out of Supreme."
Later, I saw my colleagues

carrying volumes
of Nietzsche and Marx, their bodies
looking as if they couldn't uphold
some colossal news.
And the students waiting in classrooms
for some utterly practical

invitation to the moon.
And me? From a mountain top
a man with a telescope might have said,
"His day was daylight,
office-light, dusk and dark."
I walked out into the streets again,

the sure sanity of lovers
here and there. What did it matter
that I had the shards of a song
almost put together? It was so private
so full of the present
it would elevate nothing, cheer no one.

IN THE SAN BERNARDINOS

It was boring going up the mountain,
my companions speaking of ponderosa
pines and the mid-summer snow
on Mt. Baldy. My legs didn't hurt,
I just preferred that bar in Wrightwood,
halfway to the valley, where beer
helped the talk into surprise
and the pool balls clinked
and there was no obligation to beauty.
At 6000 feet, though, a wild red
flower grew solitary and I started
to anticipate others like it
growing amid rocks in small clearings,
no pattern to them, nameless
to me, and that's how I forgot
about the too-easily-loved view
and the top I didn't want to reach
and the insistent peacefulness.
Later, going down, I felt nothing
but the declension of my own movement,
saw only the blur of green
and Virginia's sweet human backside
in front of me. What could I say to her,
who loved it all, what could I say
to any of them who wanted calm,
who preferred this thin air
to sea level's hum and complication?
And what was I afraid of, up there,
and to what couldn't I yield?
We embraced at the bottom
as if all distances were bridgeable
by touch and recognition,
the beer in Wrightwood
solved the momentary general thirst
and on the drive back our shirts
stuck to our backs, we descended
into the heat and more heat, everything
I remembered.

THE RAIN FALLING NOW

What I want to say
has nothing to do with the rain
falling now; it has fallen before
as predicted. Nor has it to do
with tears or sperm
or any effusion I can remember.
I'm thinking of a pebble, the kind
a Cambodian three weeks without food
might mistake for a soybean.
I'm thinking of hard winters and wind
moving through cattle skulls
on the prairie. And all the emptiness
inside me, luxurious, almost comic.
I hear the rain falling now
and I'd like to kick a red ball
up into the clouds and drive away.
I'd like to imagine it without me,
bouncing with ever smaller bounces,
coming to rest, wet, irrelevant.
In a mood such as mine
it's tempting to invent a clearing
in a forest, to speak about it
as if so many people before me
hadn't built fires there,
settled in to safety.
But I'm interested in the animals
that stare from the darkness,
the ones that hold back
and the grizzlies who sometimes act
like agents of the wilderness.
I want to say something
about the tremolos in the throats
of farmers as the crops come up.
I want the drought to be over
and the sky once and for all
nobody's false hope; just sky,
a perpetual accident.

What I want to say has nothing to do
with lullabies, those simple tunes,
or with what priests chant
from their code books.
I want to say that hidden
in every fist is a life-line,
that the world is just a book of maps
if you don't have money,
that nothing I say matters.
I want to say it anyway,
dumb and as insistent as rain,
go as far as I can
past that body fog, that flotation
of heart and bone, where so much
is waiting to be startled.

OPEN SECRET

We sit in different rooms, reading,
   vaguely pleased
      by the cellophane hiss

of night traffic on rainy streets.
   I'm thinking loneliness
      is a book that doesn't take us away

from ourselves. Tomorrow I'll think
   it's something else
      deserving of another definition

like the nuances of snow to an Eskimo.
   I put the book down
      and you come in

as if that were your signal,
   but you're just passing through
      on your way to the refrigerator,

lonely too, pleased perhaps
   the little light comes on
      as it's supposed to.

Outside the storm has picked up,
   making the sound we love
      on the porch roof. I imagine

a branch falling on a telephone wire
   and the wire withstanding it.
      Whoever doubts this

is a good evening mustn't know
   loneliness is our open secret,
      our Siberia from which

we are always returning.
   I go back to my book
      where the author is trying to pull

the nod string so I'll nod.
 He'd like me to believe everything
  is as it seems.

But his landscape is dazzling,
 paragraph after paragraph
  of life on the desert,

the spiders, the water inside a cactus,
 so many kinds of lizard
  one learns to make distinctions.

SENTIENCE

After midnight, that special sense
   of aloneness. The children
      breathing palpably

in their rooms. My wife's sleep rhythms
   like the movement of water
      in a full jar, a calm

that reaches down even to here.
   I'm sitting in the ugly chair
      because I can't stand

to look at it, snifter of cognac,
   night sounds, luxury of pure sentience,
      luxury of being alone

when others are nearby.
   One of the cats asks to be stroked.
      The other curls

on the sofa, *mon semblable,*
   pleased with his raspy tongue,
      Narcissus with claws.

Oh I feel such an odd sadness—
   a far away pleasure in it—
      like the simultaneity

of grief and an inheritance.
   As I turn the lamp off, the motion
      of my hand as I do it.

WHILE CUTTING THE ROPE

the knife slipped, slashing my thigh.
I didn't have enough hands or rags.
A little death arrived, I felt it,
then remembered how to make a tourniquet,
the intelligence of stopping things.
If understanding starts with a wound,
at that moment I understood
that even blood has two lives:
the red effusion, the blue, safe
undercover lie. And in this world—

so many more accidents
than choices.

At the hospital as my skin
grew together and death's visage went
from room to room, I understood the sheets
were ingenuity and labor,
the television was mysterious, amazing,
the telephone moved
the stories of our lives!
This could have been the moon.

Friends visited. I showed them
the long scar, and we spoke
of the body's fragility and its magic,
the accidents that convince us
we are little more than paper
that can be torn and burned.
We knew that wasn't profound. And yet
to say it out loud, to acknowledge it,
was a kind of pact to live
more deeply, and more lives.

Hospital talk. The conscious mind.

The scar hardened. At home in bed
I touch it now and remember the knife
slipping, the strange absence
of pain, my simple desire then
to cut the rope, to have pieces.

LATE SUMMER

It's the kind of night housecats sleep
on window sills with one eye open
and cars take corners too fast
and those teenage memories come back,
those strategies for getting home.
Or it's the kind of night
I need to remember such things,
nothing happening at all,
the stilled riot of sleeplessness
driving me to the kitchen for a glass
of water, a glass of change,
or, as someone said about experience,
"It's all true,"
and it's late summer and a late hour,
angel flowers opening to the moon,
crickets winding down to a buzz,
the cat, yes, on the sill
and me standing by the screened window
with an empty glass.
I'm thinking, "It's never too late,"
but I don't know what I mean
and I'm thinking of yesterday
at the zoo and the magnificence,
the variety, of animals
which is a sensible man's proof
that God exists,
but it's the kind of night
I'm thinking of Dachau too,
a sensible man's proof of the opposite.
I'm wondering if the moles are tunneling,
humping up the lawn,
it's the kind of night years ago
a hood named Crocker
made my face rise as if moles
had tunnelled under it all night long,
and it's a lovely night
to make some guesses about the stars,
to fill up my glass

and let the stench of sulphur
lift out of it, then drink it down,
to see what can be done about sleep
and its opposite, to listen
until I can't listen anymore
to the night birds trilling in the trees.

FAIRY TALE

There was a small house that existed
and a wing to that house which didn't.
And he had made promises
about space and had once said
something about privacy, which everyone
in the house understood to be their own.
But the wing was not just a wing,
it needed a foundation and a roof
and most of all it needed money
so he told them wings are for the rich,
there would be no wing this year.
This was when the children wept
and reminded him of his promises,
and his wife said she couldn't live
without a wing, a wing was what
she dreamed of those nights
when the house was so small around her.
So his wife took a terrible job
typing the afterthoughts of those
with many wings, and the money
was green and full of plaster
and beams and so many windows.
That was how the wing the children
call their own was built and how
the distances in the house grew larger.
He sits in his room now,
the one on the other side of the house
and his wife sits in her room
and there are hardly any accusations.

AMIDST THE FALTERING

After a sentence by Galsworthy

Amidst the faltering and the falling apart
a ship goes down, my child's ship
in the bathtub, and the world seems silly again,
all the blossoms of doom I've imagined
reveal themselves as language, nothing more,
disconnected from this oddly nice day
I find myself in,
why even the sun is almost shining!

And the woman I love with all
the normal difficulties is suddenly naked
and her hair is wet and she's twisting
the water out of it. This, after bad blood
between us, another end of the world.
The muscles in her thin arms
are young peasants shifting in church.
Her breasts, those droplets on them,
could have been stolen
from one of Cezanne's bowls of fruit.

Maybe I've finally arrived at that high plateau
where philosophy lives with despair,
where nothing can be done but know
nothing can be done.
Maybe that's why I'm laughing,
why I feel like saying Jesus Christ
over and over again, as if it were a mantra
full of amazement and resignation.

THE UNSPOKEN

Your skin has returned to its original
blushing grey, the bruise gone
into your body which will keep it
forever, beneath feeling, among the insults
and ice. Now to look at you
is to see some billboard with a history
of being marred by vandals, clear
for a while, the layers of faces under it
covered by obscenities.
But only I see this, and I'd never
say it out loud. He who hits you
for those sad, almost forgivable reasons
would say you are beautiful
and he, well, sees nothing
when he drinks too much. To the world
you are the slightly nervous barmaid
at the Black Cat whose rouge sometimes
is overdone. "Every man I've ever known
has hit me," you told me once
and I could imagine the cycle,
how you cower and say "Don't"
and he does. I'm no healer,
I just come here late afternoons,
those eternities before supper, I can't stop
myself, don't look to me.
But I've made up a story,
a bedtime story about the both of us . . .

    The empty rocking chair that rocks
       in your nightmare—there,
          I've stilled it. It's the beginning

    of a story I'm telling you
       in which a woman gives back
          her scars to the fist

    that caused them. Just gives them
       back. And when that man
          speaks harshly

this time his words fall into him,
  sandpaper all the way down
    his throat. Sit back

and listen. The curtain of yesterday
  has dropped down, it's the first hour
    once again.

This room overcast with weather
  you consider permanently yours—
    close your eyes

and pinpricks of light will arrive.
  See. You are changing as the story
    of your life changes,

my voice full of erasures.
  Someone who loves you comes along,
    that's the only twist

in the plot. I'm that person,
  I am saying as I touch you
    I will not touch you

any harder than this.
  Where the scars were: a white field,
    a story unfolding.

Listen to it,
  the luxuriousness
    of its omissions . . .

Stories end, that's my kind of cruelty.
And you can't afford to care—you're tossing
ice cubes into a glass, you know
I'm just another man in your life
who's going to walk out, good as gone.
It's to be read at night, this story.
Everything in it wants to be true.
Some day, some late afternoon
when all that's literary in me breaks down
and becomes speech, I'll say it to you.

I COME HOME WANTING TO TOUCH EVERYONE

The dogs greet me, I descend
into their world of fur and tongues
and then my wife and I embrace
as if we'd just closed the door
in a motel, our two girls slip in
between us and we're all saying
each other's names and the dogs
Buster and Sundown are on their hind legs,
people-style, seeking more love.
I've come home wanting to touch
everyone, everything; usually I turn
the key and they're all lost
in food or homework, even the dogs
are preoccupied with themselves,
I desire only to ease
back in, the mail, a drink,
but tonight the body-hungers have sent out
their long range signals
or love itself has risen
from its squalor of neglect.
Everytime the kids turn their backs
I touch my wife's breasts
and when she checks the dinner
the unfriendly cat on the dishwasher
wants to rub heads, starts to speak
with his little motor and violin—
everything, everyone is intelligible
in the language of touch,
and we sit down to dinner inarticulate
as blood, all difficulties postponed
because the weather is so good.

ESSAY TO A FRIEND IN LOVE WITH THE WRONG MAN AGAIN

It was never meant to be sensible,
fully understandable. The digger wasp,
for example, goes up to the tarantula
like a friend and the tarantula freezes,
allows itself to be inspected.
Then it digs the tarantula's grave
while the tarantula watches. You, I bet,
would have guessed with a name
like *tarantula,* the tarantula would've been
the villain. But it is we who named
the tarantula and made the digger wasp
sound honest, hard-working.
And, of course, there is no villain,
only the scheme of things, only horror,
and occasionally the strange birth
of a butterfly and its short, gorgeous,
utterly careless season.
I should have mentioned the digger wasp
doesn't kill its victim, but stuns it,
drags it to the grave, lays one egg
on its stomach, and closes up.
You see, the instinct is maternal.
The newborn wasp feeds
off the tarantula for weeks,
digs itself out at the right time
and enters the odd, wonderful world.
I've no advice for you, my friend.
You, who would take it—
as all of us would—and offer it
up to the heart, like a sacrifice.

COMING ON

On the eve of my 40th birthday
(and for Joe Gillon, dead at 35)

Death came at dusk in the middle
of a kiss, the letter said,
and there were other reports
of things ending before they should.
All day I felt the stars
before they came out, or was it
the future I was feeling,
my little unlived parts?
And now eight o'clock
not yet summer, the light
beginning to fade.
All around: the kind of quiet
that follows a scream.
And the landscape just sitting there
without me.
I feel different now, half-aware
I've taken part in some drama
in which everyone dies a little
as the protagonist dies.
Too bad the serum of love
can stop things only for a while;
and how beautiful, terrible,
none of us can make it by himself.
The night, as if this were the end
of any day, coming on.

THE BAD ANGELS

They are writing our names in the sky,
the bad angels with their calamitous wings.
They are spelling them wrong, exaggerating
the loops so that we'll see each other
askew, imperfect, like clouds broken off
from other clouds, separated by blue.

Worst part of me, old underminer
whom I've exiled unsuccessfully
into the far away charged air,
I know it's your black-winged gang.
I wish I had some invisible means
of support, some magic against you.
I wish I could marshall all
that's ever gotten away from me:
Love and loss, what plutonium!
What oblivion I could send you to.

They are changing our names in the sky,
making their own insidious designs.
I am one man with just the normal equipment,
saying No, offering little essays to the wind.
They are removing the vowels now.
They are erasing the beginning and the end.

TOWARD A COMMON PRAYER

I'll speak it personally to you
then let the wind take it and hope
it will touch those lost
in their own houses
or on Interstates
just driving, afraid to sleep.
I want it as ordinary as hers was,
my older student, who wrote
"Let me sit in the green chair,
chores to do, but no need to do them
yet, far away someone I love
pronouncing my name."
I want it to reach home
and all the way in.
Outside my window now, a morning moon.
Inside, a shoe horn
near my difficult shoes.
I'm looking all around, afraid to start,
I who've spoken prayers like a sleeptalker
without urgency or belief.
Let the woman in this prayer
be you, a survivor
of her own worst thoughts, un-
immaculate, a key to my door.
Whatever our sorrows, let them turn
into muscle around the heart.
Let there be a child so secure
she could dream of something bottomless
as she rolls down the hill.
Let there be a rare delicacy
to put whatever needs it
together again. And let the future begin
as if you were standing in front of me,
unaware of what benediction means
solemn, beginning to nod . . .

AS IT MOVES

Last week I saw a child
riding an escalator, terrified
when the steps disappeared
and I thought once again
about primitives and the next moment,

the chasm that exists at the tip
of our knowledge. I wanted
to tell the child a story
about the steps, how they
sometimes crawl on their bellies

in order to survive,
how at some safe perfect moment
they rise and become what they are.
But I moved on of course,
went home thinking, oddly,

about a different kind of innocence:
the friend I'd lost to a yoga ashram,
my cousins at the brick plant
and their wives with rosaries.
It was Saturday,

I piled the garbage in the car
and took off
for the dump where seagulls perch
amid orange rinds and broken chairs.
The dump people were out

sifting among the shards.
I can't quite explain it, but
I felt tainted in a proper way
with the world. The seagulls rose.
I wished I could tell my friend:

Look, nothing's simple.
It was almost dusk. I was thinking
the seagull is a comic, filthy bird
magnificent as it moves
upward in imperfect air.

ELEMENTARY POEM

1   There was death.
And there was the occasional touching
which reminded the body
it was alone.
And there was the weeping.
And the laughter which understood death.
And the laughter we couldn't bear.

2   There was the house or the apartment.
And there was the office
or the factory or the field.
And there was sleep.
And there was in between.
If work was satisfying
love was possible.
If we loved power
there was an emptiness that never
stopped needing to be filled.

3   There were fire, water, air.
And machines that made them ours.
There were wild things
and the things on shelves.
And there was boredom when the rain fell,
boredom on the most beautiful days.
After the pleasures came
we wanted them to come again.
And got sad.

4   There was play, our bodies in motion
forgetting they would die.
And the sudden remembering
after the sweat dried.
And there were the questions,
the old ones, over and over.
And the hard work in the yard,
the routine erasures,
the cleaning of hands.

5   There was language.
    And what had to be written
    because it couldn't be said.
    And there were the translations
    from other languages.
    And the daily translations
    of our own.
    And each thing in the world
    had a name,
    and was waiting for a name.
    And there was silence with its history
    of bad timing.
    Coming our way again.

Carnegie-Mellon Poetry

1975
The Living and the Dead, Ann Hayes
In the Face of Descent, T. Alan Broughton

1976
The Week the Dirigible Came, Jay Meek
Full of Lust and Good Usage, Stephen Dunn

1977
How I Escaped from the Labyrinth and
*   Other Poems*, Philip Dacey
The Lady from the Dark Green Hills, Jim Hall
For Luck: Poems 1962-1977, H.L. Van Brunt
By the Wreckmaster's Cottage, Paula Rankin

1978
New & Selected Poems, James Bertolino
The Sun Fetcher, Michael Dennis Browne
A Circus of Needs, Stephen Dunn
The Crowd Inside, Elizabeth Libbey

1979
Paying Back the Sea, Philip Dow
Swimmer in the Rain, Robert Wallace
Far From Home, T. Alan Broughton
The Room Where Summer Ends, Peter Cooley
No Ordinary World, Mekeel McBride

1980
And the Man Who Was Traveling Never Got
*   Home*, H.L. Van Brunt
Drawing on the Walls, Jay Meek
The Yellow House on the Corner, Rita Dove
The 8-Step Grapevine, Dara Wier
The Mating Reflex, Jim Hall

1981
A Little Faith, John Skoyles
Augers, Paula Rankin
Walking Home from the Icehouse, Vern Rutsala
Work and Love, Stephen Dunn
The Rote Walker, Mark Jarman